PROVING
IMPACT

PROVING IMPACT

Measure effectiveness and drive results

Andrew Jacobs

Copyright © 2024 by Andrew Jacobs

All rights reserved. No portion of this book may be reproduced, copied, distributed, or adapted in any way, except for certain activities permitted by applicable copyright laws, such as brief quotations in the context of a review or academic work.

For permission to publish, distribute or otherwise reproduce this work, please contact the author at hello@llarn.com

Book cover by Llarn Learning

First edition 2024

For Natalie

About the author

Andrew Jacobs is Founder and Chief Executive Officer for Llarn Learning. Known for innovative thinking about learning, training and technology, Andrew has significant experience in a range of roles across learning, training, talent, and people development.

He has a specific understanding of developing online and digital solutions for learning, social profile, and engagement.

He received the Internet Time Alliance award for his work on informal learning in July 2020 and was highly commended as part of the DHSC team at the CIPD People Management Awards in 2021. He was part of the team that won the Gold Award at the 2022 Learning Awards for the work with Capita and the DHSC and won the Bronze Award for Learning Professional of the year at the same event. He was made a Chartered Fellow of the CIPD in 2024.

You can find his blog posts every day on lostanddesperate.com and he produces the podcast Women Talking About Learning.

Acknowledgments

The are thousands of people I could list here to thank for their support, inspiration, and all-round brilliance over many years. If your name isn't here but you think it should be, you're probably right.

I really appreciate all the help I've had, particularly from:

Fran Harrison, Michelle Parry-Slater, Andy Lancaster, Heidi Kirby, Dr Alaina, Szalatcha, Loren Sanders, Lior Locher, Martin Couzins, Donald H. Taylor, Anna Svitak, Nana Amoa-Buahin, David Hayden, Sharon Green, Martin Baker, Simon Gibson, Julian Stodd, Laura Overton, Naureen Wilson, Deirdre Bond, Bob Price, Michael Osborne, Jo Cook, Erica Falmer, Jane Hart, Jane Bozarth, Rachel Burnham, Helen Bailey, Tom McDowell, Sukh Pabial, Paula Hughes, Sharon Claffey Kaliouby, Gaelle Watson, Helen Hill, Kate Graham, Nick Ribeiro, Arash Rezaei-Mazinani, Piers Ansell, Anita Gouveia. And all my family for their unwavering belief and love.

PROVING IMPACT

Contents

Preface .... **Error! Bookmark not defined.**

1. Changing expectations 5
2. Measurement principles 14
3. Measurement strategy 35
4. Bias 48
5. The IOOI Model 64
6. Input and Output 71
7. Outcome and Impact 81
8. Reporting 97
9. What next? 110

Preface

In the last decade, learning and development (L&D) has changed exponentially. As much as the workplace has changed, the demands placed on L&D teams have changed too.

This is detailed in the way we work. In the past we were a supplier of content for our organisations. We produced a range of 'stuff' which people would engage with – or not.

We're moving from supply driven practice to a demand-led profession.

A demand-led approach requires a different mindset and style in the work we do.

This means our design, delivery, and evaluation must change to reflect modern workplace demands.

The redesign of learning is being accelerated on a daily basis with the development of AI solutions which have moved content creation from an art and science, into a consumer style product. You want a video? Here's a range which you may use. It's got to the point where suppliers are now able to produce whole online courses with content, quizzes, and images from AI.

Delivery has also moved on. The Covid-19 pandemic moved more people to be digitally resident and experience learning in a range of ways we hadn't thought about before.

Evaluation and people measurement haven't really shifted though.

If you described your people measurement practices now, what would you say about them?

Are they modern, reflecting the way we work and learn now?

Or are they based in theories and practices first suggested in the 1950's?

The ways we measured training and learning in the past, with event-led reactive practice, have become more and more obsolete.

Pause and think about a new graduate employee in your organisation. They are younger than Google.

They are digitally resident; their lives are blended in online and offline, and they will expect that from their work, and by association, their learning. They have grown up with access to information at their fingertips and the expectations they have from a work perspective are very different. Consequently, the ways we capture data, and report on it, need to reflect this change.

This book is quite short and doesn't pretend to solve every issue with L&D measurement and evaluation. It also assumes you have some experience in the L&D profession and a little background in the way L&D works.

At the end of each chapter there is space for you to think about what it has said and for you to reflect on the content from your context.

What I hope these will do is give you pause to consider what you do now and how successful it really is.

If you want to develop yourself further in this area, visit llarn.com for further details.

1. Changing expectations

When I started in the world of work in the late 1980s, a lot of L&D was 'just in case' learning.

Just in case learning exists in organisations to provide learning 'just in case' someone does something, and we can prove they were 'trained' beforehand. This approach still exists today in compliance training where we harvest the data of completions. This is used as an attempt to prove people did the training they were meant to do. Just in case learning is about raising people's awareness of things they already know and mandating it to demonstrate they did the 'thing' we needed them to.

There's nothing inherently wrong with just in case; this approach is a bedrock of a lot of the compliance, onboarding, and mandated learning in organisations. What it does to L&D's detriment is create an appetite for completion data.

L&D has pleased the organisation by reporting back on who did what, how they scored, how many times they did it, and the rates of completion across the organisation. Again, there's nothing inherently wrong with this approach but it becomes the expectation from managers and leaders that 'this is what L&D does'. If you're only ever asked to present completion data, all you'll ever present is completion data.

With the move to improved technologies through the ages, we were able to create just in time learning. Just in time learning started with audio and video tapes and moved through the 1980's into laserdiscs, computer based training, and digital content.

Just in time learning suits organisations because it is highly scalable. For example, instead of getting people in to show colleagues how to lift things safely for manual handling training, it can be produced once in a digital format, and re-published many times. Just in time learning is easily measurable if your measures are simply completion data. Based on platforms, L&D functions can craft content to be accessed through one portal and this makes the completion data much easier to collect.

Just in time evaluation reporting was a little more problematic for organisations until the introduction of the Learning Management System (LMS). The LMS enables organisations to collect transactional data about employee completions of eLearning. When a standard set of technical standards were released - Sharable Content Object Reference Model (SCORM) – it meant we could capture and download reports at a moment's notice.

This responsive approach again pleased our organisations; we could get data to them quicker and when they asked for it – just in time reporting was becoming a thing which L&D could use to amplify our purpose.

Content expectations have changed

There is, however, an issue here. As the image above shows, there has been a bigger shift in L&D, and just in case and just in time don't meet the ways people want to learn.

'Just for me' learning is more complex. People realised, with the advent of mobile technology over the last few decades, they were able to do the learning they wanted, at a time which suited them. With increased accessibility, people discovered new content away from the central L&D platforms in your work and business. For example, Excel courses are rarely facilitated face to face now since YouTube can take you to the bit you need to learn in a matter of seconds. Access to online accessible content is also repeatable, readily available, and outside L&D collection practices.

Having fluid timings meant L&D functions had to prepare more 'menu' based content to try to move people back to their platforms.

For a while this worked.

Then the COVID-19 pandemic moved the needle even further away from organised learning. Just enough learning became even more critical as people, often separated from their work teams in remote spaces, started self-determining what they needed to learn. This meant even more chunking down of learning content.

A course, which might have been made up of several elements, was now split into smaller and smaller chunks and we found people learning at much more flexible times, locations, and for different reasons.

Is it any wonder it's difficult to measure the effectiveness of people interventions when it's more than 'just a course' anymore?

The same applies to the way we report our measurements and analysis. If there is an expectation that people can learn differently, the way we have reported learning activity won't cut it any longer.

The just in case leader wants to be able to access all the data and insight whenever they need it. This is what they are used to since this is what the learning function has provided them with for the last few decades.

The just in time leaders want to know they can call on the learning function to tell them what they need to know at a moment's notice. Again, leaders are used to this since we have a LMS to produce reports. Whether the reports add value is moot; they are still, in many places, just a list of people having done a 'thing'.

The just for me leaders want to know the impacts in their area of work. It doesn't matter who else has done things. They want to know about 'their' people and the most useful activity they have completed and 'learnt'.

The just enough leader doesn't need to know that 78% of participants scored a GPA of 4.2; they want to know that the intervention has improved their people's performance. This seems for many people in L&D to be an unobtainable goal – providing just enough data, personalised to a manager, to prove the impact of the learning on their team's performance.

So, L&D are being asked to prove their worth more but we're facing shrinking resources, distributed models, and technological innovations which have changed the expectations of what we do.

It's no wonder L&D shy away from evaluation practice; if we can't prove any impact we are seen just as a cost.

Let's take AI for example. Apparently, anyone can now create documents, video, audio, courses, and quizzes just using the technology we have available now. With limited control over production of this material, and the way these tools have been democratised, L&D functions are being left behind.

Against these backgrounds, we need to think differently about what we measure and how we report it, and for that we need a strategy.

Think about your learning offer.

How much is just in case, just in time, just for me, just enough?

How does this affect your approach to evaluation?

2. Measurement principles

You probably turned the page expecting to see a chapter on strategy here.

To be completely honest, this book was initially written that way, but I realised we need to address something before we can start on our strategy, and that's the principles upon which we need to base our measurement approach.

It was a while ago when I understood we needed principles supporting a measurement strategy. All the learning strategies I see are based on specific principles; this might be organisational values, professional standards, technological guidance etc.

What I rarely see are principles describing what good measurement and evaluation practice should be. In many cases, the approaches we use are highly transactional, detailing the way data will be captured, but not how data will be woven together to turn this fibre into fabric.

One thing I have seen a lot in the past decade is the reach that learning is making towards marketing. We see marketing principles in our learning design and understanding of how to 'sell' initiatives to people. So, I went searching in the marketing space and found the Barcelona Principles.

The Barcelona Principles refer to the Barcelona Declaration of Research Principles, a set of seven voluntary guidelines established by the public relations (PR) industry to measure the efficiency of PR campaigns.

First drafted in 2010, they were revised in 2015 and in 2020. The Barcelona Principles were the first attempt to create a framework for effective public relations and communications measurement.

Having a common understanding in the language of measurement cannot be overstated. Agreeing a set of principles which we can take outside of the L&D function and discuss with our peers across the organisation is essential.

We've become stuck in models and processes and continue to count the wrong end of the person. I used the Barcelona Principles as inspiration to craft some alternatives which, I think, create a common language between the learning and people functions and the rest of the organisation you work with:

- Goal setting and measurement are fundamental to workplace learning and development
- Measuring learning performance outcomes is always recommended versus only measuring outputs
- The effect on organisational performance can and should always be measured
- Measurement and evaluation require both qualitative and quantitative methods
- Learning cost figures are not the value of learning
- Social learning can and should be measured consistently with other learning activity
- Measurement and evaluation should be transparent, consistent, and valid

Let's interrogate each of these principles, work out what they mean, and try and help translate these into ways of thinking about evaluation in the workplace.

Goal setting and measurement are fundamental to workplace learning and development

Goal setting in this context should not be the goal of the learning function, but the business goal. We spend too much time working out how we can prove the value of the learning function by counting lots of 'things' – bums on seats, eLearning completions, happy sheet averages, etc.

By starting with a business aim, business performance becomes a key indicator of the effectiveness of the learning activity and function. This could be uncomfortable for many in L&D; how can the function be held accountable for the individual and team performance. I'd re-frame the question to ask, what are you doing if you're NOT measuring your effectiveness through individual and team performance?

Haven't got managers on side? Work with them to understand what they really need and that means changing the dialogue of provision to one of demand.

For example, a request for a customer skills course should be used as an opportunity to uncover what measurable business outcome is the aim. If it's a customer retention target, the aim of the learning should be built around that, and measures put in place so the target can be checked. If it's about reducing call waiting times, a quantitative target should be agreed.

A business goal isn't optional, it's essential to the commercial focus of an effective learning function.

Reset the conversations with your business. Ask them what the business problem is they're trying to fix and how they'll know if it's fixed. They'll think of your L&D function very differently.

Measuring learning performance outcomes is always recommended versus only measuring outputs

What do we mean by learning performance outcomes?

I've asked this question dozens of times in the last few years, and it seems to be a bit tough for people to pin it down.

One way I've come to describe it now is to ask for the difference between what happened in the training and learning activity and what happens next.

Learning performance outcomes are not outputs. It is not the numbers of events, people on courses, course completions, or evaluation form scores. It is not 'engagement' with content (however that might be measured), activities started, favourable comments received or test scores.

Outcomes are what happens because of the learning event happening and should be measured in performance terms. We'll look later in this book at the differences between learning data and performance data but here is an example.

Compliance training is an area we mention regularly in terms of output data. You can probably tell your sponsors the numbers of courses completed, pass rates, and the functions which complete their training first in the financial year. This is output.

Compliance outcomes will be demonstrated in performance terms through activity such as compliance breaches, budgetary control, and key controls. Outcomes will come from what you can measure that affects product cycles, quality control and assurance, and risk management. These are outcomes.

Outputs describe busyness; Outcomes describe business.

The effect on organisational performance can and should always be measured

This probably seems really obvious, but if you can't demonstrate that your activity as a

L&D function has any effect on the performance of the organisation, why are you there?

If you don't know the effects of what you do on your organisation, you're not doing your job.

This principle creates an explicit reason for the learning function to work with the rest of the organisation to identify the benefits of the work of the L&D team and the impact it has.

I speak to L&D teams who are afraid to ask this question. It's not that they don't affect the performance of the organisation, but the fact they start asking the question might put their head above the parapet. If that happens, can they defend themselves when asked to prove their impact to the rest of the organisation?

One way to work round this is to start asking business related questions of your sponsors.

When they come to you for a management course, ask them what they expect the impact to be on the organisation's performance. Ask them how they'd like that to be measured and reported. Ask what they believe the benefit to be and if they don't know suggest some options.

If you're developing managers, ask how they expect customer service to improve because of this management programme, if it relates to new customers only or existing customers as well. Ask what measures they have in place, and can you see them before designing, so you can make sure the intervention you design is targeted specifically at these relationships.

The other way to manage the flak which will come is to prove the effects of what you have been doing. Not in output terms but outcomes.

Report back on the managers who have spent time developing their skills in managing their teams, have improved employee wellbeing and been more successful.

If you don't have examples, go and find them now.

Measurement and evaluation require both qualitative and quantitative methods

In an interview with the Guardian newspaper in 2017, the late author Hilary Mantel described her research and how she interpreted the evidence she uncovered:

"Evidence is always partial. Facts are not truth, though they are part of it. Information is not knowledge."
Hilary Mantel 2017

We currently see use of both quantitative and qualitative approaches to collect low level data for learning and development. These are the common happy sheets which populate our profession, ever evolving, yet always staying the same.

We rely on these to present people with a semantic differential scale, usually a numerical option between one and five.

Occasionally we'll list words:

Awful - Poor - Average - Good - Excellent

Innovative design in this space has previously relied on scales of one to six (no middle marks), emojis (more fun), and other dalliances with 'amusing' presentation.

Qualitative data has been generally in the feared 'Comments' section where users are asked to describe the experience they have been through. In some cases, these are in the form of questions which are unerringly answered in generic and limited ways.

For example, look at the list below of typical questions and responses:

Q. What did you enjoy?

A. All of it.

Q. What would you change?

A. Nothing.

Q. What else do you want to say?

A. Thanks.

These forms do little to shift the perception of the L&D function as people pleasers. When our colleagues challenge these clichés, we smile, shrug, and suggest we can't do anything else.

There is data in opinion, but we need to collect it differently. It needs to be done in the workplace where a range of other people can provide a range of views.

Think about children playing a musical instrument. They pass the quantitative levels for their assessments and work their way up through grades. However, place a bunch of these children together and ask them to perform in concert together, they will all bring a different approach to what they're playing. The conductor sets the direction of these children, maintains the narrative, and can hear all the performance.

L&D needs to be the conductor.

Learning cost figures are not the value of learning

I'll admit to it, in the past I've used the cost of learning to demonstrate the investment being made in people in the organisation I work for.

In some cases, it's to highlight how much is being spent to prove that people matter, and the high costs are a justification for expensive courses, classes, workshops, and technology.

Similarly, I have used the drop in spend to prove the low costs are a justification for alternative provision, nil/neutral cost development activity, and a frugal approach.

The problem with focusing just on the cost means you are, quite rightly, judged as a cost centre.

$$\text{Value} = \frac{\text{Perceived Benefit}}{\text{Cost}}$$

Look at the equation above. There are three variables which we need to understand. Before you can talk about value you need to have absolute clarity about what is meant by perceived benefit. Go back to the earlier principles and you'll find references to outcomes, performance, and business goals.

Start talking about these in your organisation and people will change what they want to talk about and how they want to approach value. How would these fit into your approach to evaluation?

Look at the costs in REAL detail. That means both the direct costs AND the indirect costs. Direct cost should be easy to quantify; look at the expense put into your platforms, materials, facilitator costs, design costs, etc. Indirect costs will be productivity related and include time out the office, opportunity cost, fail rates, etc.

Value never equals cost.

Social learning can and should be measured consistently with other learning activity

I mentioned earlier I had come up with these principles a few years ago. I've spoken about them at several conferences and events, both face to face and online, and this principle is the one which receives most criticism, confusion, challenge, and misunderstanding.

At its core, social learning theory posits that people learn from one another through observation, imitation, and modelling. Albert Bandura emphasised that people could learn in a social context by observing the actions of others and the outcomes of those actions.

L&D has always had a problem with social learning. Look at the following list of 'informal' learning activity and think back to how you have measured them in the past:

- Shadowing
- Mentoring
- Meetings
- Cross functional work
- Projects
- On the job coaching

How many of these forms of learning would the L&D function be measuring?

Social learning in the workplace is a dynamic and integral component of professional development. The networks, communities, and spaces we work within are brilliant places for people to acquire knowledge and understanding.

At an even simpler level, the Post-it note stuck on a screen which labels where to plug a laptop in, is a form of social sharing which we rely on as intrinsic in our workplaces.

How can we count this then? The key is in what we share, where we share it, how often we share, who we share with, and why we think it needs to be shared.

We'll look at sharing later in more detail, but it won't be about your LMS or other platform. This isn't the 'Field of Dreams'; if you build it, they **won't** come.

Your colleagues already have channels where they share but which L&D are probably excluded from.

How we access, engage in, and get value from those channels is how we can capture social learning.

Measurement and evaluation should be transparent, consistent, and valid

Again, this seems like a no-brainer as principles go. However, what is your approach to evaluation for your onboarding, Health and Safety and Leadership Development programmes? Are they the same, or do we place more weight on some L&D activities?

If you're going to take these principles forward, you must do them cohesively and across the organisation as a whole. That means everyone needs to be aware of what data you're capturing (transparency), on all the programmes you cover (consistency), and the data you're using is relevant to the work you've done (valid).

Transparency is about clarity in the process. People will buy-in as stakeholders and users if they understand performance is also being measured. It lays the design process open and creates space for people to highlight the elements they think are needed. Most importantly, it builds trust between the learning function, the individual, and the line management.

Consistency helps to ensure fairness across the organisation in both in the learning approach, and how we collect and capture data of performance. It benchmarks performance of people going through the programmes L&D creates and, as importantly, holds the L&D function to account.

Validity means measuring what matters and makes sure methods used to review performance are capturing the intended outcomes of the learning activity. Data based evaluation informs future strategies, allowing L&D to prioritise what really matters.

You have seven principles from this chapter and probably need to reflect on them a bit.

They have been described to me as motherhood and apple pie; they appeal to common beliefs; indeed, how many of them are difficult to agree with?

When you've thought them through in the context of your organisation, you'll need to start to socialise them across your organisation. That means starting to talk to managers, peers, senior leaders, and people across the organisation.

What you want is to seek their comments and thoughts and understand their position in each of these principles. It is likely they will agree with them in general.

This agreement is essential.

Before agreeing any strategy, people need to know the underpinning assumptions you are aiming for with your new measurement strategy.

Look at the 7 principles again.

Which would be the easiest to bring into your evaluation strategy in your organisation?

Which would be the toughest?

How might you overcome this?

What additional principles might you need?

3. Measurement strategy

Someone once described me as a learning strategist – it's a title which has come from working with organisations on their learning strategies.

I'll be asked to come in and help support teams through changes in their practice and refresh their approaches. I'll often find extensive thought has gone into the supply process for learning and the technology stack which has been – or will be - deployed. Similarly, the delivery channels and andragogy will be well researched and extensive marketing and evaluation plans will be in place.

When I ask about the measurement strategy, that's the time when one of two things happen. Often people look at the floor and under their breath mumble things like 'we don't have one'. The alternative is the raft of happy sheets and transactional data which has been captured and will be reported on.

As mentioned before, the way we learn has changed and our strategic approach to measurement, evaluation and understanding of our effects and impact must change too.

This isn't a simple list; this is a change to the way you think about evaluation.

If we plan so long on crafting custom content, aimed at individuals and teams to make them the best they can be, why don't we do the same with evaluation and assessment?

Look at the figure below:

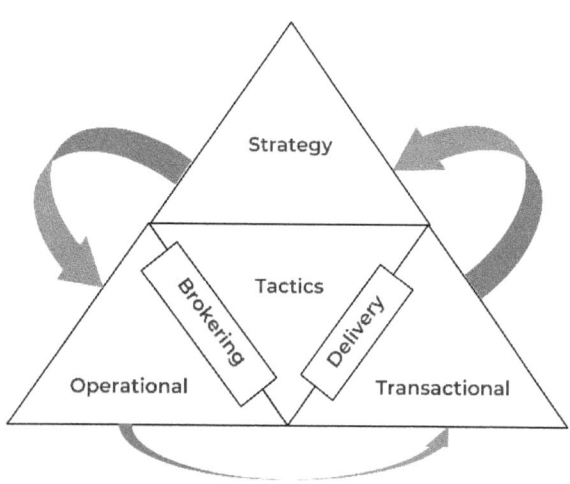

This is an example of what happens in L&D too often. This image represents what we see as the 'conspiracy of convenience' in L&D. We are tasked with a strategic imperative to '**do something**'. This thing we do creates operational work for us which, since we haven't been involved in the problem analysis fully enough, creates lots of action.

But when challenged, we can say we have **'done something'**. This activity is then completed by the organisation who complete the activities and present us with lots of transactional data proving **'they did the thing'**. They were asked to **'do something'** and did it. We then report this back as an example of strategic metrics.

What's wrong with this approach?

Firstly, it isn't strategic. It is operational and transactional, relying on simple input and output metrics which, as we described in the last chapter, are not as effective as outcomes. These metrics are evidence of doing a thing, but not whether it's the 'right' thing.

Secondly, by working outside this triangle, we are not working tactically.

When working with organisations on their strategies, I spend a lot of time reminding L&D leads they need to think strategically and act tactically. As you can see from the image this opens two further fundamentals – brokering and delivery.

Brokering is the space where you demonstrate how the principles we discussed in the last chapter will work. The principles are your permission slips to act tactically and are essential to create agency for you to do things differently.

We've already mentioned the measurement principles we went through in Chapter 2. The principles will underpin the approaches you can take and, if socialised effectively. will give you agency to develop an innovative and comprehensive strategy. Making this strategy work is delivery.

The second element to work on to create an effective evaluation strategy are the 3 Bs – Build, Borrow, and Buy.

Let's look at each of these in turn.

Build

Of the list of the 3Bs, build comes first for a couple of reasons. Firstly, you want to demonstrate you have the skills and resource to change your approaches. Secondly, you don't necessarily need to buy more resources, platforms, or technology if you already have these systems.

I regularly see this with L&D teams; they have technologies and platforms which are not being used to their full capacity. The capacity exists to get a different level of data, but this has not been investigated in the organisation. This will partly be down to a lack of understanding about data analytics.

If you're a large organisation, where is your Learning Analytics and Evaluation Centre of Excellence? An enterprise size organisation should have a consistent approach to evaluation and standard processes for collecting data. If you're a micro enterprise, what are your data skills like and what gaps do you have in your knowledge?

Building isn't just about creating processes and systems, it's about your knowledge and skills too.

As part of your build, invest in upskilling internal evaluation capabilities. Who can provide comprehensive training and development opportunities for L&D professionals to build expertise in areas such as survey design, data analysis, storytelling with data, and change management? Look internally first and create a culture of sharing for nil/neutral cost.

As well as data collection, look at how you can engage with people in the organisation to build expertise in areas like data analysis, and storytelling with data.

I'd guess you've used design thinking approaches to your L&D practice – do the same for evaluation. Look for the human-centred design principles. Find a way to prototype new approaches rapidly and refine them iteratively.

The last suggestion I'd have for building is an evaluation data governance policy. Your principles will be the foundation of this policy and, if your organisation likes guidelines and protocols, work through what these will be like.

Borrow

One problem with borrowing elements for a good evaluation strategy is there aren't many REALLY effective approaches out there. If there were, we would be seeing them at every industry event. What we do see are innovative ways to track learning completion data with gaps between learning performance and operational success.

In Clayton Christensen's book Disrupting Class, he identifies four interdependencies which are expensive and limiting for anyone seeking to innovate.

One of these is lateral. As described in the book, it suggests that you can't teach modern foreign languages in a different way because this would mean teaching English in a different way. This form of 'best' or 'accepted' practice means that anyone doing anything differently to this will be working outside of the cultural norms.

This limits innovation in L&D because it floats the idea that the way things are done is approved and accepted in specific ways only, and anyone doing something will be sticking their head above a parapet, creating an opportunity to be shot down.

So, the first thing we should be doing is benchmarking against the L&D industry, L&D peers, and leading organisations and finding the people who are strategising and working outside of the 'conspiracy of convenience'. Seek out the outliers who are working above the transactional and operational and looking at outcomes and impact.

I spent years looking at who was successful in several fields and have dozens of evaluation case studies where people have presented their findings. None of these are in the L&D space; seek out who is linking the work they do to outcomes sometime after their activity has completed and look at how they build the links between the different parts of their work and the way they capture data.

Similarly, seek out the case studies which **don't** demonstrate sound evaluative practice and see what the gaps are.

All these approaches mean looking up and out. Find the industry forums, conferences, networks, and Communities of Practice (CoP) where people are stretching their practice in evaluation. It's really easy to be sucked into an echo chamber where we assume the things we're hearing are right – bear this in mind in the next chapter.

Within the principles, we mentioned sharing as a key way to detect social learning activity; the same applies to measurement. Find the people in your organisation who are doing good things using evidence which you can work with to promote good practice.

Buy

Part of the conversation any L&D team has with suppliers needs to focus on evaluation and measurement. However, we look at buy last when we're looking at an evaluation strategy. The expectation of doing less with more is a presence in many of our organisations and we need to make sure we are using our systems to their fullest.

Later in this book we will look at some techniques and places where we can expect to find data; you might need to think about what your current platforms and providers can do and what they need to be able to do to support you fully.

If you do have to buy in tools, you need to make sure they don't duplicate what you already have, are evidence-based and, most importantly, cost-effective.

Procuring tools which make things look nice but don't add depth or breadth to your data collection and insight are of much less benefit than the unassuming but effective data store and algorithmic inquiry.

Make sure you have clear criteria if you need to purchase support. This should include things like the compatibility with your existing systems. Don't accept a 'yes we can' response unless it's followed with a 'yes we can show you'.

Make sure whatever you choose and develop is compatible across ALL your learning platforms and ecosystem. If there is one product which doesn't fit, you will always be having to add that in which will be both frustrating, time-consuming, and prone to error.

Regularly check out what's happening in the market. That means actively seeking out evaluation techniques, services, and technologies. Your approach can only be up to date if you understand the latest industry research reports and trends.

Lastly, work with your current suppliers and vendors to customise solutions to fit your needs. Proving value for you is in their interest and benefit, as much as it is yours.

You will now have agreed principles and have the start of a strategy in place. Ready to start collecting data?

Not yet. Before we do, let's have a look at one of the ongoing issues with data capture and reporting – bias.

> Make a list below of the parts of your evaluation strategy you need to:
>
> Build
>
>
>
> Borrow
>
>
>
> Buy

4. Bias

Let me say at the start of this chapter, I am not an expert in statistics or mathematics. I have a basic understanding of statistical analysis, but I do understand the pressures and biases that L&D feels – and reflects – in the way we look at learning and evaluation data.

Similarly, I am not an expert in psychology. I do know, however, there are over 180 cognitive biases which interfere with how we process data, think critically, and perceive reality.

What I do have is three decades' experience in the learning industry and experience of thousands of L&D professionals wanting to prove their worth.

There's a great scene in Spinal Tap, one of my favourite films. In it, the interviewer (Rob Reiner) asks the lead guitarist of the band – Nigel Tufnell – why his amps go to 11. Apparently, it's because it's one louder than 10. When asked why he doesn't make 10 louder, Nigel replies – 'but it goes to 11'.

Nigel is, of course missing the point; the volume the listener hears will be the same, it's just his belief it will be louder.

There's a lot of this bias in L&D; we work in an industry which focuses on the input we create, and we measure that to **our** standard, rather than the individual's standard. Consequently, we rely on our approaches over the effect they create.

As we've seen before, the desire to be seen to do something pushes us to collect data which, in many cases, we use to justify our busyness. This is one bias we adopt in L&D and is called **impression management bias**. At its core, it is about making the L&D team appear to be more successful, have a bigger impact, or just plain 'nice' to have around.

There are dozens of other biases which we can also fall into when we are collecting data to demonstrate we are measuring effectively. In this chapter we'll look at a few of the common ones and try and help you understand why they happen and what you can do to make sure you're being as objective as possible.

What we can't do is correct those biases for you; you need to review them and consider how you might need to mitigate them in your work.

Pattern sensitivity bias makes us focus on evidence that confirms our existing beliefs. We see this regularly in L&D through the commissioning of courses, classes, and workshops. They've always 'worked' before, so we commission them again. We follow the patterns of previous activity and assume it will be appropriate to simply repeat what came before. We don't, however, have any specific evidence as to the success of these approaches, so are commissioned on the assumption they'll work.

To reduce pattern sensitivity bias, consider:

- Structured data analysis. Using two independent sources (and evaluators) will make your assessment more objective.
- Diverse perspectives. Look for a range of sources and opinion. Diverse viewpoints

challenge assumptions and uncover potential biases.
- Pre-established criteria. Design clear evaluation criteria and rubrics. A rubric framework keeps the evaluation focused and objective, reducing the influence of pre-existing beliefs.

Acknowledging pattern sensitivity bias is the first step to understanding how it impacts your data collection.

Attribution error bias appears when we want to find success (or failure) and are led along a path which shows us convenient explanations. We roll a programme out and observe a spike in managerial effectiveness which must obviously be down to the training. But it isn't. The learning intervention will be one part of a range of events and activity which will be happening in an individual's life, and we need to look at that performance in the context of the individual. When you start collecting different data to prove impact it takes time, skill, and understanding to recognise what is actually happening and respond and report that.

To reduce **attribution error** bias, the first step is to accept it and that means working out what impact your L&D support truly has. That means being unafraid to highlight what L&D doesn't do; what difference do your onboarding courses really make?

To reduce attribution error bias, consider:

- Examining your data. Look for confounding and contra indicators. Seek out the differences in your data points and use those as your base to investigate what happened. We want to find causation between your activity and the business impact so work out where it doesn't happen.
- Control and comparison groups. Use the power of having control and comparison groups to isolate effects. By contrasting the outcomes of participants against those who did not undergo a programme, L&D can more accurately attribute observed changes to the intervention itself.

As with pattern sensitivity bias, the simple fact of knowing you have a problem will begin to shift your attribution error biases.

Self-importance bias is an inflated sense of the importance or impact of L&D work. Allied to attribution error bias, we can overstate the significance of our findings and make sweeping recommendations that aren't fully supported by data. This is common in new programmes, or shortly after programmes are launched as we attempt to prove we've made a difference. It's understandable; we want to prove the thing we've produced, commissioned, delivered, has had an impact on where we work. If we don't prove it, we're at risk of challenge as to our effectiveness, so we naturally look for the benefit.

To mitigate self-importance bias:

- Encourage peer review and external validation to check your findings. Using SMEs and external stakeholders in the verification process will start triangulating your work.

- Recognise what the evaluation can't check. That means being honest about what you know the intervention is unlikely to impact on.
- Find specific changes in actions. Where people can directly relate performance to learning, celebrate it, but make sure you also look for where expected change doesn't happen.

Having humility and knowing you aren't changing the world is a key foundation to remove self-importance bias.

L&D is full of **allegiance bias**. There are a range of learning theories, approaches, and practices which have, for some time, led the way we work. These come from a range of places and take hold as the preferred way of doing things. For example, we regularly see studies stating both sides of the argument about whether face to face learning or online learning is more effective. They are, of course, highly contextual, but if it is the interest of a practitioner to recommend one way, we will seek those allegiances in the data we collect and analyse.

To challenge your allegiance bias:

- Maintain an open mindset and consider alternative learning theories. Different approaches favour different contexts and understanding these perspectives will make you a better and more modern L&D professional.
- Know your limits both theoretically and practically. Just because your design and technology **can** do something, don't try to fit those results to the elements and thinking which you have invested your time and money into.
- Anchor your evaluation in the aims and outcomes of the programme. As we'll see in the next chapter, performance data is always going to be more useful than learning data.

Keep your attention on the skills which are demonstrated by the programme, rather than a theoretical debate on why something should work.

One of the most common biases I see in workplace L&D is **availability bias**. It happens in almost every course, class, or online activity. We place a short form in front of people after the event and ask them to rate/review what they have completed. We do this very shortly after an event and it is impacted by availability bias. This bias is a mental shortcut that relies on immediate examples that come to a person's mind when reviewing a topic, concept, method, etc. If something can be recalled, it must be important, or at least more important than alternative solutions not as readily recalled. Consequently, **our** content, event, etc are the most relevant and useful.

There are a couple of ways you can mitigate availability bias:

- Collect and analyse data over an extended period, rather than relying solely on recent or highly publicised events. For a significant learning programme this could – and arguably should – be over months or years.
- Focus on trends over anomalies. Trends follow data points over an extended period and can be increasing, decreasing,

or stable. They are, however, consistent. Anomalies, on the other hand, tend to be indicators of errors, unusual events, or potential areas of investigation. While recent events deserve attention, L&D need to look at the trends in performance over time to identify the overall impact.

Acknowledge the potential for availability bias by explaining to your sponsors and stakeholders what a **realistic** timescale will need to be in place to find out what really changed because of your work.

I've seen plenty of **courtesy bias** in workplace learning and it is pervasive, affecting the way we try and prove impact. At its most simple, we see it with participants wanting to rate the learning activity they have completed favourably. This is done to keep the L&D function happy and avoid further interventions or prevent conflict. By adding a favourable score or comment it justifies the time away from the working environment and supports the line manager decision to offer the support to the individual. It is also done out of politeness and to avoid offence to the facilitator, designer, supplier, etc.

The second way we see courtesy bias is more dangerous. This is when the L&D function report the 'good stuff' to avoid confrontation with sponsors. Looking for the positive metrics, L&D seeks out relative performance improvement. For example, being 20% better than the previous year, being 8% above the industry standard, and so on. What this does is hide the shortcomings of the L&D function and only serves to store up problems until the day someone interrogates the data.

Ways to overcome courtesy bias include:

- Using anonymous or confidential data collection methods to encourage honest and candid responses. This can help with large scale programmes where intimate investigation of individual performance is unlikely to be required.
- Being absolutely clear about the importance of honest feedback. This is an opportunity for people to share criticism in a way which can directly affect future

programmes and activities. This will significantly shift the learning culture in your organisation.
- Using multiple data sources as we've mentioned before. Look for additional learning metrics, e.g. completion data, as well as qualitative metrics. We'll look at these in the next chapter.
- Working with stakeholders, to focus on solutions. Acknowledging that little or no impact has occurred can be framed as positive actions and solutions. Explaining how things didn't work will help you broker and design better future support, rather than just providing vanity metrics which make no difference to the organisation.

Agreeing evaluation principles, socialising them across the organisation, and co-designing and co-creating measurement activity will substantially help alleviate courtesy bias.

The last one I'll mention in this chapter is **pro-project bias**. This comes from the desire that we have in L&D to please the people we work with and for. We want our approaches in L&D to be successful, engaging, and fun, and seen to be effective and innovative. We put our energy into crafting what we think are excellent activities, content, and support for people. It's understandable to want to emphasise positive findings and hide negative aspects of our work. Unfortunately, the consequences of pro project bias in L&D evaluation can be costly. We continue with programmes which should have been withdrawn. We pay for technologies, systems, and suppliers who, since we have an investment, we want to prove are successful. Flawed evaluation can perpetuate ineffective learning support and mask what's really happening in your organisation.

We can mitigate pro-project bias in a few ways:

- Engage independent who have no vested interest in a project's success or failure. Their objectivity can ensure a more critical review and appraisal of an intervention's effectiveness.

- Develop a culture of objective and critical evaluation within the L&D team. Your evaluation principles – as we discussed before – can help set the tone and temperature of your evaluation methods and build practice which celebrates constructive criticism.
- Consider blind review processes where one team evaluates another team's work. This can be done in-house, cross functionally, or, if you're really brave, seek out external co-operation on a nil/neutral cost basis to validate your work.

Again, acknowledging the potential for pro-project bias is a first step. You can build trust in your work and function if you are honest with yourselves and the people you work with about the effectiveness of your work.

As I mentioned at the start of this chapter, I am not an expert in statistics or psychology. What I can do is highlight the most common mistakes I recognise when I see organisations want to evaluate their work. Indeed, I've fallen foul of some of these biases myself.

The desire to please and prove your worth **will** skew your thinking and the ways you evaluate.

This is why the principles I mentioned in Chapter 2 are so important. They establish the ways evaluation will work in your organisation and start to create the environment where people can view, connect and constructively criticise the effectiveness of the L&D function.

This is a different way of working and thinking about the way we evaluate, and it might take some time for you and your organisation to both understand your biases and find ways to mitigate them.

In the next chapter we'll look at what this means in practice and help you build an approach to evaluation which challenges some of these biases and build on the principles you've agreed internally.

There are 188 recognised cognitive biases. How do they impact your work?

What have you done to mitigate them?

What else do you need to do?

5. The IOOI Model

I like to tinker. It comes from when I was a kid; I used to take toys apart and try to put them back together, or more likely, integrate them somehow. Think Toy Story's Sid Phillips but much less violent. As I've got older, I've updated laptops, built PCs, and played with settings on things to see what else I can use something for. It's something I've carried on into my working life – I play with ideas and put things together to create new and alternative ways of thinking about L&D.

I've been thinking about evaluation in L&D for a while. It's been over ten years and has, for that time, been an itch I haven't been able to scratch.

I've thought about principles, bias, and strategy but have never been able to put them together across a simple model to be able to describe the spaces and places where the rich data exists in L&D evaluation.

One day, I was reading about the success of an approach in a social care setting and reference was made to logic models. I tracked back and forward and came across a whole subset of approaches to evaluation I had not worked through before.

Logic models can be traced back to the 1970s and were developed to try and work through the challenges in measuring the effectiveness of projects and programmes.

Over time, they've been used across sectors like education, public health, and social activity. I have probably come across them in my public sector work, but I never made the link between them and learning.

Logic models are usually made up of the following key steps:

- Inputs
- Activities
- Outputs
- Outcomes
- Impacts

I realised that the 'Activities' step might easily be re-labelled as 'Learning'. By doing so we would have four clear steps and places where we might look to capture evaluation data.

Input data

The input data is the data which we use to identify how and when people access learning. For example, we might want to know if people have been mandated to attend or have volunteered. Similarly, how many times do people access the learning activities we create? When working on a national programme in the UK, I found that users accessed the platform where the content was hosted 3.1 times. The immediate questions I asked were why, and how long did each entry last.

Output data

There is immediate tangible data of the learning activities. For example, this would describe the proportions of content completed. What we rarely do in L&D is then associate this completion and output data with what happens in the organisation. In your output data, you'll find reflections and qualitative feedback; it's essential we collect this along with the quantitative data – as we mentioned in the chapter on principles.

Outcome data

Outcome data is the 'so what' data from the activity. It's great we can track what people were invited to and completed, but knowing what happened afterwards is really important. We'd expect to see changes here which will kick in after someone has been back in their workplace. Outcomes might happen very quickly – we can see a more informed colleague making better decisions immediately – or over a longer period of time as people adjust their skills, knowledge, behaviour and attitude following some time back in the workplace.

Impact data

This represents the long-term, broad changes which we will see in the organisation. These metrics are, like the outcome data, not held in the learning function and reflect the performance of your colleagues in the workplace. Built into the context of the organisation, we would find performance data here, such as improved productivity, employee happiness, and customer satisfaction.

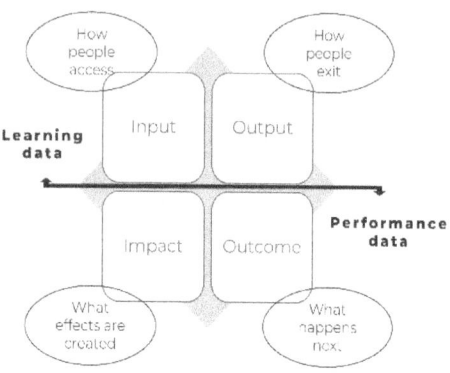

So here are four definable areas where we can capture data. You'll note that our input and output activity will produce learning data; in isolation, learning data provides no evidence of any impact on performance. To get to the 'good stuff' we need to work out where to find outcome and impact data and that is found in the performance metrics of the organisation.

In the next couple of chapters, we will look at sources for this data and help you work out where you might be able to prove your impact from data sources in your organisation.

Start thinking about the data sources you currently use to inform your evaluation.

See if you can identify them as input, output, outcome, or impact sources.

6. Input and Output

As we saw in the last chapter, input and output is data which we'll be able to collect from the L&D function.

What we don't do is collect this consistently as we saw in the principles. Part of the problem with doing this is having absolute clarity about what data we have and **could** and **should** record.

I've worked in L&D for a long time and have spent a lot of time trying to simplify the data we might collect. I've found people like the theory of good practice, but L&D professionals love a list – I know I do. So, here are the five main occasions and milestones when we can start collecting input and output data.

These are:

- Entry
- Content
- Sharing
- Exit
- Reflection

Within each of these areas there are some key metrics which are worth looking at. Let's review them in the order above.

Entry

Within entry, we are looking at how someone comes to the learning activity. For example, someone who is mandated to complete a learning activity is likely approaching it differently to someone who has voluntarily entered. Similarly, it's useful to see who sent the colleague here; was it a manager, peer, family, or friend? This matters to validate the effectiveness of sharing and we will come back to it shortly.

Someone's whole journey can be framed around how someone appears on the L&D radar. I'd question whether we do this sufficiently now.

Also useful is knowing how many times someone enters and re-enters their learning support. For example, as I mentioned earlier, the large project with the UK government, users visited the platform an average 3.1 times each. When we knew the reasons behind these multiple entries, it made it easier for us to design the resource appropriately. Knowing **why** people access is incredibly useful data for L&D.

Content

Content refers, quite obviously, to the content which people might access. What is useful for the learning function to understand is which parts of the content are most popular. More important is knowing which parts of the content are most useful. On the programme I mentioned before, we had over two thousand people access a Welsh language section. It was popular but of almost no use to the people who logged into it since we had fewer than two dozen Welsh speakers. Why did people access it? 'Because it was there' and 'I wanted to see what it was about' were the most common responses.

Knowing which elements of content are completed, in which order, is an essential step here. A core issue for people working in L&D is the sponsor or SME who assumes that everyone needs to know everything. A key function of modern learning is creating space for people to personalise the support they need. Knowing which activity people complete helps the L&D function curate the most appropriate resources for people with a similar background.

Share

Over the years when I've mentioned this as a metric, I find people are surprised and sceptical about how this data might be tracked.

One way which is available is to add sharing buttons on your LMS/LXP but the number of people who use those will be limited. It's estimated that between 10 and 20% of users leave feedback on Amazon; how many are likely to share a learning asset with someone inside the workplace from a platform?

We need to recognise where people share now and make sure L&D is in those channels. For example, in organisations who use Microsoft, find out who shares what on Viva Engage. Finding the people who are serial sharers on 'outer loop' social tools is useful in finding the influencers internally. The same can be said for Teams – track down the people who have social influence in the organisation. These people are the people who shape and form the learning culture in your organisation, and you need them to be on your side.

What really matters with share data is knowing the effectiveness of social sharers. Take two colleagues – Alex and Baylor. Alex shares 100 elements a year and 3 or 4 people respond and react. Baylor shares 20 elements a year and 16 or 17 people react. Both are sharers you need to have in your organisation but knowing WHAT they share and with WHOM is essential to be able to track social learning practice.

Exit

Exit data should be simple to measure, at least on your digital platforms. Knowing when someone left and how long they were there should be easy to track.

How often people return though, and where they go back to, is incredibly useful to know. It is likely an external event prompted them to go back, and knowing what that was, and how the content was reused, can be helpful in your design approach.

Understanding the performance of people through assessments, quizzes, and assignments should be useful output data, available on exit. It's not, however, a knowledge test. Peer assessment is incredibly valuable here and it's simple to create. Ask a previous cohort to assess the current cohort. This creates social engagement, spaced practice (for the earlier cohort), and assessment once an individual is back in the workplace. You will get clearer feedback and an expectation that the current cohort will now become the assessors for the next team.

At exit, we should also be looking to see where people go next. Having clarity on the places people go, who they connect (and share) with, and what they value next is useful when you come to curating your offer.

There is a problem with capturing non-digital exits. We can all probably remember the coaching which fizzled out and the mentoring which just stopped. The exits and ending from analogue activity also need to be tracked and they are, most often, found in the last area on the list.

Reflective

Reflective data is what L&D generally collects now. It's the qualitative records we capture through happy sheets and feedback forms. We often retain, summarise, and, in rare cases, even report on it.

The modern L&D function recognises reflection takes place outside of the L&D space so it's important to find out who people reflect with; there's that sharing again.

Knowing what feedback they offer, to whom and where, should be part of the L&D approach as much as the design and delivery. As I mentioned earlier in the book, there is a limit to how much people will share on a happy sheet and the value in offering alternative channels is incredibly useful. For example, creating a channel for managers to feed back as part of their post learning briefings is a simple way for managers to record their thoughts, and for L&D to collect useful data.

The useful reflection happens after your colleague has gone back to their work and is either chatting with their peers or managers. Ask your line managers to include feedback about learning as part of their regular team meetings. This data will be structured and regular, creating capacity for you to record what people think when you're not in the room.

As I mentioned before, this input and output data is useful to work out what people want to learn and which elements they use but we really want to find out what outcomes we produce and the impact they have.

> Look at the 5 areas identified in this chapter – entry, content, sharing, exit, and reflection.
>
> How good are you at looking at these 5 consistently?
>
> How well do you analyse and report the data?

7. Outcome and Impact

Outcome and impact data is the holy grail for many in L&D, yet, if we agree principles and a strategy, it shouldn't be.

As mentioned earlier, this is the performance data which is created when we see what happens next and what effects are created by learning interventions. As we saw before in bias, there is a fear in looking for this data and finding nothing. This is partly because we don't have a structured list of places to look at. Again, I've been thinking long and hard about this for some years and have drawn together the following list of data capture points you might want to look at:

- Baselines
- Repetition
- Control Groups
- Estimation to Reality
- Context
- Qualitative
- Business Performance
- Business Result

As we did in the last chapter, there are some key metrics in each of these areas which are worth looking at. Let's look through them in the above order.

A quick note though; you are not expected to do all of these – it would be excessive and counter-productive. You do, however, need to start with the first on the list which is essential in every measurement activity you undertake.

Baselines

We often hear about having the end in sight when we're looking at learning design and delivery, and the same should be carried through in evaluation practice. It's as simple as asking what expected change is required. The key point here is that this is **NOT** a learning change, but a performance change. Too often, we are engaged to develop an individual, team, or function, and the baseline is an omission of learning or training. We then fill that gap, and this activity creates a new baseline, full of learning objectives. If you want to demonstrate outcomes and impact, you must look beyond learning objectives, and understand the performance aims.

Within performance baselines, you want to understand the starting point, the end point, and the milestones along the way. This is essential so your work remains active throughout the whole process of learning and performance. These milestones should be performance led and informed by other items in the list above.

We need to make these baselines SMART – Specific, Measurable, Achievable, Relevant, and Timely – since these are the measures we will be judged to.

Repetition

How long does it take someone to become 'competent'? I think a lot of L&D has operated under the assumption that people are pushed into 'learning' at one end and come out fully formed trainees, competent to do every task.

What makes commercial pilots and firefighters competent, is the work (and by association, learning) which they complete after they have finished their training. A potential pilot will need to complete 1500 hours as a first officer before they can move seats and call themselves a pilot. Similarly, a wholetime firefighter will take 18-24 months working at a fire station to be declared competent. When leaving their training environments, they will be proficient; when they have completed workplace activity, they will be competent.

It might seem like semantics but if your sponsors are expecting fully formed individuals after they've left the learning function, they will be continuously disappointed by your work. This is why the repetition of task and performance in the workplace is so important. L&D's role should be to work with supervisors, managers, and peers to understand the time to competence and this only comes about through repetition of performance in the workplace.

This is more than a reputational issue – it goes to the heart of L&D as a development function.

If the perception of the learning function is that you deliver entirely competent colleagues at the end of a process, your stakeholders will be disappointed. By maintaining the approach we do that 'learners' will be 'competent' we will continue to disappoint.

Control Group

It can be incredibly useful to compare cohorts. Every person brings something new to a learning experience and process, and each cohort will be different in composition as a result. However, being able to compare the performance of a group who have experienced L&D intervention with a cohort who have not will immediately create points of similarity and contrast.

In workplace learning and development, evaluating the effectiveness of new training programs or interventions often involves the use of control groups, like A/B testing methodologies seen in research and marketing. This approach allows organisations to make more informed decisions based on comparative data, enhancing the strategic implementation of future training.

You need to take care when selecting groups to compare. It is unethical to withhold training/learning from a group purely for the purposes of evaluation, so using pilot programmes and comparing new approaches with existing activity is a good way to start.

Data collection in control groups should focus on quantitative variables and you need absolute clarity on any differences between groups at the outset.

Despite these challenges, using control groups has significant benefits. They provide a clearer picture of how effective learning can be by directly comparing outcomes between those who received the L&D interventions in one way and those who did not. This is incredibly useful feedback to those in L&D when you're analysing and deciding how to refine and improve future training interventions.

Estimation to Reality

This focuses on comparing initial estimates of performance against the actual results achieved. It's impossible to measure this performance metric without having agreed at the start what the baselines are.

As we mentioned, we need these to be SMART so we can measure them objectively. Part of your baseline process might be timebound – will that programme take three, six, or nine months to become effective? They might be quality focused – do managers make quicker and better decisions now than before? They might be a combination – how long an individual needs to be shadowed for.

This area also requires clear understanding of the pace and cadence of performance. L&D need to make sure any data collection is tied to the frequency and rhythm of performance checkpoints in the workplace. Make sure you're speaking with interested parties when they've spoken together in reviews, debriefs and team meetings.

Making sure you're engaging regularly will make your future estimates more reliable, and keep you connected with workplace performance.

Context

Cinema was once described by the US film critic Roger Ebert as "a machine that generates empathy". This is because what you bring to a film, cinema, video, etc will affect how you feel about the film.

The same can be said for learning; take new manager development, a staple of pretty much every learning function. If I'm new to management, I'll be approaching this with a specific background and focus. If I'm new to management in this organisation but have experience as a manager in other organisations, I'll perceive the programme differently. Similarly, if I'm an experienced manager but new to management in the sector, my view will be different again.

We wouldn't expect these participants to come to the event the same, and we shouldn't expect them to get the same from the support.

Robust evaluation will understand the different contexts where people are performing and consider that in their data capture and reporting. A manager with one direct report and a team of four will have different challenges to put learning into practice than someone with three reports and a team of twenty.

Similarly, our function, work programme, location, customers, etc. will all have a direct impact on people's performance, and we need to be able to understand this context to evaluate effectively.

L&D need to pay more attention to the fact that content is king, but context is kingdom.

Qualitative

A brief reminder from Chapter 2:

Measurement and evaluation require both qualitative and quantitative methods

This principle applies to performance metrics as much as learning metrics.

We know we can track quantitative performance metrics, but it would be sensible – indeed expected – that we look at qualitative metrics from managers, peers, and (where appropriate) teams.

The effect of a manager on someone's performance can't be underestimated; role models for behaviours, tasks and development, the manager is in the best place to give feedback to the individual – and the L&D team – about the individual's performance.

It is essential – as we saw in Chapter 4 – that we consider bias and prejudice from the line manager. Were they the person who insisted on the learning activity and why? If they're approaching from a position where the individual hasn't been performing, we need to consider that in our recording.

Most importantly is to make sure qualitative feedback is consistent and structured. That means you have clear guidance which describes the process to all parties and is focused on specific, relevant criteria from the performance. These criteria **must** be related to the learning activity.

Business Performance

When I talk to people in L&D about reviewing business performance as part of our interventions, they can feel a bit uncomfortable. We are called on when there are failures, e.g. Health & Safety, compliance, etc. Why shouldn't we be claiming a part of the pie when we can demonstrate a link to the successes?

Business performance isn't necessarily the financial metrics – we look at them next – but the other elements which will be impacted by a change in performance.

These fall broadly into 3 categories.

The first is employee and colleague metrics. Depending on the learning being supported, these might include employee survey and satisfaction results, absence, grievance, or other employee data. Employee and colleague metrics will review skills development and employee retention. Employees are less likely to leave an organisation where they feel they are being developed. It is worth looking for innovation and creativity metrics, as well as succession planning effectiveness. Diversity measures such as Gender and Ethnicity Pay Gaps can also be useful metrics here to support the learning team.

The second category of business performance the L&D team should be reviewing is internal controls, audit, and governance. The key controls in the organisation will be reviewed in this category and include measures such as compliance and audit. In addition, L&D should be looking at process efficiency, i.e. how well tasks are completed, and quality control – are products and services to standard? Cost management and budgetary control fall into this category and will include performance elements affecting the organisation's budget from learning activity. For some industries, this will include stock management, inventory, supply chain management, and utilising capacity.

The third category of business performance we should review is the effect on the customer. This includes both internal and external customers and might need to reflect the impact on new and existing customers. The L&D team might want to review customer satisfaction scores and net promoter scores (if your organisation uses them). If you work in a sales space, the customer acquisition cost and retention rates might be an area you wish to review. Similarly, customer service response times and complaint/compliment rates will provide a wealth of data for the L&D team. Purchase rates, additional purchases, and engagement levels are all areas you might want to look at to review the L&D team's impact.

Business Result

After looking at the range of results, contexts, performances, and feedback above, we get to the bottom line. What effect does the L&D team have on business performance? It **should** be simple to answer but without having investigated the areas in the input, output and outcome sectors, it will be a challenge.

What I can't do here is list what this will be for your business – each person reading this book will be working in a different organisation and sector and the results for one organisation might be completely irrelevant for another. For example, private sector metrics like earnings before interest and tax (EBIT) and gross profit will be unrelated to the government sector where programme reach, and sector specific measures will be in place. Similarly, the third sector will be considering metrics like donor retention rates, service delivery and fund utilisation ratios.

Over the last two chapters I've listed the 13 places you can start to collect data and information from to start to analyse and figure out how the work you're doing is having an impact. What I strongly suggest is that you **DO NOT USE ALL OF THESE**.

It is neither practical nor appropriate to find data across all these sources. What we need to do is understand what will work for you and we look at that in the next chapter – reporting.

> Look at the 8 areas identified in this chapter. Which would be the easiest for you to start collecting and how are you going to make that happen?

8. Reporting

Your head is buzzing. You've seen there are at least 13 places where you can start collecting data and want to start reporting back from. A reminder of these:

Input/Output	**Outcome/Impact**
Entry	Baselines
Content	Repetition
Sharing	Control Groups
Exit	Estimation to Reality
Reflection	Context
	Qualitative
	Business Performance
	Business Result
	Baselines

As I said at the end of the last chapter, it is **really** tempting to start collecting data from all these sources. This isn't, however, good practice. As well as creating a substantial increase in work, it's quite possible – indeed likely – that all these sources aren't relevant for your purpose.

So where do you start when you come to reporting?

Before you start collecting and analysing, remember the stakeholder expectations on evaluation and reporting will be different. As we saw in Chapter 1, there has been a shift in how people want the content we produce. The same applies to evaluation reporting.

Evaluation expectations have changed

In the past, L&D was able to report busyness and the numbers of completions; in the new world of learning and data, we must be able to prove more and in a range of formats and demands.

That means being clear with your stakeholders about your reporting process and agreeing clear expectations with them. To support this, it is likely you'll need to understand the following elements about each of the evaluation types you'll need to report:

- Value to the sponsor of this approach
- The critical success factors for this reporting
- The key challenges for the L&D function
- The essential activities the L&D function needs to complete

For **just in case** evaluation, your sponsor will want this reporting to confirm that activities are being completed to meet their compliance reporting requirements. For example, we collect the numbers of people and rates of completion of fire safety training to meet the requirements of Fire Safety Orders.

The critical success factors for this type of reporting are simple. The first is whether it proves completion of learning activity. As I mentioned at the start of this book, we love to provide this data since it demonstrates our busyness, it's easy to count, and simple to report. The second success factor is having the data available to be reviewed. Just in case evaluation is usually reported to a schedule so we can prepare in plenty of time.

The challenges for just in case reporting are primarily about getting people to do the thing we want. Getting people to complete the required activities, whether that be online, or face to face, and, to pass the assessment at the end of the activity, is L&D's biggest challenge. This is partly because it can be difficult to keep people engaged when they are repeating 'learning' which they may have completed many times before. The final challenge for L&D with just in case reporting is being able to record consistently. This is why we rely on simple tests, quizzes, and scalable questions.

We can improve just in case evaluation. Firstly, vary the assessment approaches which you use. Relying on the same content and same assessments is monotonous for users and it can be easily updated. Using formative assessment, for example, and only offering the required content to meet the mandated score can significantly reduce user time. The second and most important way to improve this form of evaluation is to be unafraid to making management accountable for completion, rather than the learning function. This shifts the accountability within the organisation, and if the reporting requirement can also be sent to the audit functions responsible for completing the compliance activity, even better.

With **just in time** reporting of evaluation your sponsors want to know they can get the information when they need it urgently. It's likely they will need a lower level of data than for just in case evaluation. For example, with this approach you'll be expected to be able to pull accurate data very quickly for reviews, hearings, grievances, etc.

The critical success factors for just in time reporting are twofold. Firstly, being able to pull the data on request means it needs to be live (or as near to live) as possible. This means that your supplier must be able to confirm your system is always ready and backed up when needed. The second critical success factor is making sure you're collecting up to date information. With content and eLearning hosted on your LMS, this is relatively simple. The difficulty comes when your colleagues and users are completing activity 'offline', or outside the LMS. This creates a few challenges for the L&D team.

The biggest challenge for you and your team is making sure the data you have is accurate and, where necessary, verified. I mentioned the 9th principle is about transparent, consistent and valid; this challenge faces this straight on. As well as accurate data, you need to overcome the issue of extracting the data in an easy way. Many suppliers of LMS technology have improved their extraction and reporting tools. Make sure you can do this with ease before purchasing a learning reporting tool.

There are two key activities which the L&D function should engage in to support just in time evaluation. The first is to make the reporting tools accessible by the users. There are two reasons for this: firstly, the L&D function don't need to gatekeep the data and it makes much more sense for the managers in the business to access the information they need at a time they need, and not wait for the learning function. Secondly, and more importantly, it demonstrates to managers that this data is transparent and available whenever they need it. This shifts the stakeholder/sponsor expectations of the learning function and improves the reputation of the L&D team. The second activity the L&D team need to do is build a reporting timetable for the organisation. Identifying the dates, months and quarters when specific information is required means the team can plan for collection, analysis and availability for reporting.

Just for me evaluation is when the line management in the organisation doesn't care about what's happening outside their function and want to focus on how 'their' people are doing. This means being able to supply and analyse information about teams, working groups, projects etc.

The critical success factors for this approach are based on the relevance of the information supplied. This is where the L&D team,

having understood the baselines of the
programme, are able to supply the
appropriate data. Making sure you are
collecting performance data which is relevant
because of the learning activity is incredibly
powerful. Similarly, being able to provide
individualised reporting to managers and
sponsors here is essential. Managers do need
to understand performance in context but
want to know about their teams first and
foremost.

Building just for me reporting is challenging
for the learning function. Sponsors will often
want what has been available through just in
case and just in time reporting, and want it
returned in a preferred format. I've spoken
for some years about 'Mexican food' in
learning – the same ingredients folded
differently – and this applies to just for me
evaluation. All the elements are there but
knowing how much to add or remove for
each manager requires editing and
negotiation. The additional issue over just for
me reporting comes through anonymising
data. At a micro level it may be relevant to

identify individuals, but at scale, should senior managers need to know granular detail about each element an individual or colleague has completed?

To improve just for me reporting, you need to have absolute clarity over the relationship between learning and performance. Being able to prove that what people learned created performance outcomes and had an impact on how people and the organisation works are incredibly powerful. Reporting these within the just for me space will add to the standing of you and your team. The other element to improve just for me reporting is demonstrating the impact of performance outside the performance group. I said previously that managers want to know how 'their' people are doing. By proving what happens, the effects created, and the space where this performance happened, the learning function moves to being an engineer and not just a course and training supplier.

If you ask your sponsors what data and information they really want, it's most likely to be **just enough** reporting. It's probable the managers and teams you are reporting to don't want to know that people rated the joining instructions highly; this is about shorter and streamlined reporting for specific demands of the sponsor.

There are two simple critical success factors with just enough reporting: making the reporting business specific, and being targeted at specific business issues. Business specific means tailoring your reporting to the organisation or industry, explaining the overall business context and addressing the broader organisational needs, i.e. the context. Targeted to specific business issues means focusing on individual problems or challenges, is narrow in scope, and aims to resolve pain points, i.e. the content.

The challenges in meeting these is making sure not to oversupply the sponsor with too much data. This requires skills in editing, auditing and presenting. As Allan Little of the BBC once said in a training video for news journalists:

'Simplicity is the key to understanding. Short words in short sentences present the listener or reader with the fewest obstacles to comprehension.'

For example, my shortest blog post was once only one word. It was titled Brevity. The post read:

Matters.

Interpreting the right data and analysing it requires some skill. The learning function can help themselves if they start to report widely. Taking a just enough approach, focused on the simple reporting, tailored to people, demonstrates the L&D is an analyst, an engineer, and has an eye on the business – you're not just pushing courses any more. To make this work, you **must** make sure the principles I covered in Chapter 2 are socialised, accepted and agreed across the organisation.

Reporting is the skill we too often fail at within learning. As you can see, it requires skill, nuance, commitment, and holds together all the other parts of the process. As we'll see in the next chapter, you now have a choice about how you want to take things forward.

What are the challenges you have moving from just in case reporting to just enough reporting?

How do you mitigate them?

9. What next?

At the start of this book, I mentioned I've been thinking about this stuff for a LONG time, and I want to congratulate and thank you for getting to the end of the book. There are lots of ideas and thinking here which will take time to digest and reflect upon.

That leads us into what I call the power of 10.

I first came up with this idea a dozen years ago and have found it works to focus the mind and attention on making sure things are followed through.

The power of 10 is considering these three questions at these three intervals:

>   10 days later   So what?
>   10 weeks later   Now what?
>   10 months later And what?

10 days after an activity is a generous amount of time to consider what has happened. Attending a workshop, a coaching session, a masterclass, or completing an online course, it's likely people will have forgotten some of

what they did but what we want to know is what they did remember, apply, and reflect on.

After 10 days you want to connect with people and ask them a few questions. These might be through simple questionnaires although, with more substantial programmes, focus groups or face to face interviews may be relevant.

We need to find out their **initial reflections**. It's useful to find out 10 days after an activity, what has stood out to them most. This might be the most memorable element, the biggest gap they've realised, the further activity they've carried out, or the conversations they've had.

Finding out about their **struggles** is useful to establish whether there are gaps in their ability, or gaps in their capacity to bring changes through.

Asking what **reminders** people need from the content is a good idea here. Most people will have taken notes or remember parts of the material they've covered but asking what they might want to be prompted about brings it back to their attention.

10 days is a good timeframe to ask about the **impact on work**. We'd hope to see the person's routine has changed. What does this look like and if not, what are they planning to do?

Lastly, it's good practice to create some reflection about **future outlook**. Asking during or immediately after an event how the person anticipates things will change is unlikely to be of much use; 10 days afterwards they will have taken time to consider how to integrate processes, practices, and skills into their work and should be able to describe what this will look like.

10 days after the event, activity, or action we're beginning to collect output data – see Chapter 6. This will be helping to justify the learning activity and provide us with feedback on the learning function. Remember, this is learning data – data which is easily collected by the learning function to

identify how people have entered and exited the learning we have supported. We would want to identify quantitative learning data here as well – how much content did people use, revisit, assess, etc. This is also a great opportunity to collect sharing data. As part of their reflection what did they share and with whom?

A little later –10 weeks after – we're now getting interested in performance data and what happens next.

10 weeks after we need to be considering now what, i.e. what are we seeing differently in the nature of the person's and team's performance.

Firstly, we want to tie the review at this point back to the learning activity so asking people to **reflect on goals** they might have set is a good way to start. After 10 weeks we'd expect people to plan for doing something differently – this may be unlikely in some of the mandated 'learning' we produce. However, having this data is useful to assist in future design and deployment.

It is also likely that users and colleagues will be **adapting strategies** from the learning input. It is almost impossible to replicate the real-world environment in a learning setting, so asking how the learning is being applied and moderated and revised to workplace practice is both useful feedback on the support, and evidence of the learning being used.

Establishing how people are **collaborating and sharing** their new or revised practice is a good way to establish the spread of performance change.

At 10 weeks, we should be able to see the **effectiveness of changes** in work or performance outcomes. Asking directly focuses the conversation back to performance as the driver for the learning. As mentioned previously, L&D wants to be recognised for improving performance and engaging in conversation like this will help promote our approach.

It's a good idea to ask about **unexpected outcomes** 10 weeks after. These might relate to skills or capacity but will add depth to your reporting. If there are none noticed by the individuals, don't be afraid to look wider, interrogating other data sources.

Lastly, you'll want to start leading people to think about the **organisational impact** of their learning on their work. This might be self-reported but, again, triangulating the data will prove effective. For example, if a team has redrawn their approach to coaching and performance management in the last 10 weeks, how has that affected some of the business performance metrics (Chapter 7)?

10 weeks after we are firmly in the performance space; performance data should be demonstrating positive – and negative – impacts from the learning activity. This is the prime opportunity for the L&D function to demonstrate its effect and capture stories, experiences, and information which it can use to help shape the narrative of the evaluation piece.

This is more than an after-programme review; we are looking specifically for performance change and working out what has happened and what **will happen** because of the L&D function's intervention.

It is possible – indeed probable – you may complete several 10-week reviews throughout a long-term programme. By continuously referring to the performance and re-framing the learning activity as the enabler, you're establishing an ongoing relationship with performance of the organisation.

10 months after we are firmly looking in the 'and what' space to establish the impact of the activity people have completed.

For simpler activities, this is where we collect data on multiple participants. For example, if 500 of your employees have completed Health and Safety training, we'd expect to see the impact on the organisation, and this is why we need to follow up.

Looking at effects which have been created after 10 months means that most of the data you're looking for will be performance related.

The first area you'll need to look at is how learning has been **integrated into organisational processes**. Did the management programme effect any change in the way work was done? We'd expect to see critical core skills learning having an effect of how the organisation operates. Learning you have supported around innovation, creativity, efficiency, leadership, and organisational effectiveness will have changed the way things are done. If they haven't, you need to go back to the principles you've agreed early on with your sponsors; did they **really** want organisational change from your work?

At 10 months you'll be able to identify **strategic impact on organisational goals**. How have the performances of individuals, cohorts, and teams improved the performance of the organisation? We're looking here for a clear integration of the learning approaches in the organisation and the performance. Have the long-term mission and objectives been a consistent thread in performance and have they changed because of the work of the L&D function and your attendees and users?

We would expect a **cultural shift and sustained change** after 10 months for some L&D work. Again, for management and leadership programmes, this should be self-evident. However, look at your support for other programmes; we'd expect to see how your customer approach has changed if you have been working on customer service initiatives. Similarly, we'd expect a shift in compliance, audit, and consistently more efficient processes and systems if you have been working on quality control and process learning.

The L&D function should be seeking out the **impact on talent** in the organisation. We regularly hear that organisations want to develop a learning culture and develop their leaders. This will partly be learning data led, e.g. attendance rates, but much more importantly we should be looking at turnover, pipelines, promotion and internal successes. Again, this is more likely for bigger programmes only, but all people related skills learning can furnish results here.

The last essential element after 10 months is identifying the **future strategic initiatives and capability building**. It is almost certain that you will be planning for the next 12 months and having this data and information at this point is both timely and relevant. It means that benchmarking – a key element for the L&D team's work (Chapter 7) – can be started and used to plan and prioritise future strategic approaches.

We have used the power of 10 here; the periods reflect what most people commonly want to use. You can adopt these in your organisations and feel free to amend the 10 to any other number; some people tell me 6 or 7 works. However, this will have an impact on the breadth and depth of the data available to you and may limit your reporting capability.

Similarly, some people have adopted 14 days, 12 weeks and 10 months; the numbers don't necessarily matter. What is important is that you are – as we said for the seventh principle - being transparent, consistent, and valid.

What next for you?

You'll get the option to start making some notes on this for your work and produce some power of 10 plans. What will you be doing in 10 days, 10 weeks, and 10 months? And will you be able to identify how this book has helped?

Please do get in touch and let me know what differences this book has made. Similarly, please do let me know where you disagree; this is one of the reasons I like to work in L&D and discuss approaches and activity with smart people. The L&D profession is incredibly smart, but we don't do our best in demonstrating that by crafting weak evaluation.

There is plenty more that might have gone into this book. For example, having templates for reporting would be well used. What would, of course, happen then is everyone

completing identical evaluation reports.
Again, in L&D we like seeing what works
and making that the new way of doing things.

Proving impact is much more than new
happy sheets and reports. It goes to the heart
of what we do in L&D.

If you do want to know more, please feel free
to contact me.

> Take a moment to pause and reflect on what you've just read. Your task now is to identify how your practice is going to change.
>
> In 10 days, what are likely struggles and reflections you'll have?

> In 10 weeks, what will your plan look like to introduce the content you have read into the way you measure data?

> In 10 months, what will your evaluation approach look like and how will you be able to measure its change to the culture and performance of the organisation?

www.ingramcontent.com/pod-product-compliance
Lightning Source LLC
Chambersburg PA
CBHW070142230526
45471CB00002B/482